Embrace
Your Fears
with
AWE

Jane Kucera

Embrace Your Fears with AWE

ISBN 978-0-9741318-1-8

Acknowledgments

Thank you, God, for the nudges to write this book on fear. I had been toying with the idea of another book. My past editor suggested that I try writing a fiction book. I did, and have two children's rough drafts in the drawer, but for some reason, this didn't seem the time to bring them out. I kept praying and asking for guidance. I heard the word fear come out of my mouth quite frequently. It surprised me for I didn't think of myself as a fearful person. Little by little, I began to compile the list.

I am grateful for the twelve-step program and attendees who have encouraged me on my journey by their openness.

Thank you, Shawna Reidy, for your openness in our daily writings. You have been a friend, showing me by your example of thoughtfulness how to affirm and love others.

Thank you, my brother, Bill, and sisters, Dolly, Suzanne, and Mary for your occasional question, "How's the book, sis?" and their many prayers.

Thank you, everyone—Barbara Boyd, my friend and spiritual mentor, Suzanne Battos, my one-hundred-watt light bulb sister, and my most affirming husband Don—for reading the first draft.

And dear Catherine Battos, my niece, *thank you* for all the hours editing, not just one time, but twice, and even challenging me with some of my fears. You are such a blessing to me. I am grateful.

Table of Contents

INTRODUCTION _____ - 1 -

FEAR OF BEING HONEST _____ - 3 -

FEAR OF TRUSTING PEOPLE_____ - 8 -

FEAR OF TIGHT SPACES (CLAUSTROPHOBIA) - 14 -

FEAR OF GETTING LOST _____ - 17 -

FEAR OF APPEARING DUMB _____ - 25 -

FEAR OF MY HUSBAND DYING FIRST _____ - 29 -

FEAR OF THE UNKNOWN _____ - 37 -

FEAR OF NOT BEING GOOD ENOUGH _____ - 44 -

FEAR OF LOSING MY FAITH _____ - 49 -

FEAR OF GOD_____ - 56 -

FEAR OF AGING _____ - 62 -

MY CLOSING THOUGHTS _____ - 67 -

ANGER (FEELINGS) QUESTIONS _____ - 69 -

Introduction

"Faith and fear both demand you believe in something you cannot see. You choose!"

~ Bob Proctor

I never thought of myself as a fearful person. I don't see myself as a worrisome person either. Generally, I will act and then let go of situations. If a problem lingers, I pray and trust that God will handle it. But then I read a book that talked about fear and gave a number of examples. I paused while reading each one, questioning whether I, myself, had that fear. To my surprise, I identified with quite a few.

When the writer wrote about hesitation reaching out to others, I had to admit *yes*. Other fears began to surface, such as getting lost while driving in a big city or going the wrong way exiting a building, especially with a revolving door. Another fear question dealt with finances to which I could relate. Fear of public speaking got my attention. Fear of marketing my prior book came to mind as well. Fear of God was another named behavior. Fear of being dumb and not having the answers came to the forefront of my mind. Fear of my weight being out of control has been a struggle for years. And lastly, fear of the unknown kept me from beginning this book.

I have used various writing approaches in my life when facing fear. Years ago someone gave me the list of *Anger (feelings) Questions*. At the back of the book, I have listed the questions. And at the end of the chapter *Fear of Appearing Dumb*, I give an example of my using the *Anger (feelings) Questions*. After naming my feeling, the questions help me clarify the situation. They have been a wonderful gift, a gift I would like to share with you now.

What I have come to see is that only by naming my fear, sometimes writing about it from a descriptive approach of color and intensity, and where I am holding it in my body, will I then in prayer embrace it. I have at times also written a dialog with fear, asking what it wanted of me, what it wanted to tell me. Sometimes I have seen fear wanting to help me become a stronger person, but that happened only when I embraced it and walked with it.

Was it hard? Yes! Living in fear stifled me. I want to live carefree. I have come to see the benefit of journeying through fear by taking action with God's help and grace. Courage is needed to walk through fear, and that is my prayer for you.

How to Use this Book

The following fear-chapters are a random collection. Hopefully, as you read the book in whatever approach you choose, you will be able to identify with one or more fears and be guided to unearth your own source to address. If you peruse the table of contents, one fear more than another may grab your attention. Let your emotions guide you.

As I was summing up my first fear, I noticed this symbolism: AWE – **A**cknowledge, **W**rite, **E**mbrace.

Fear of Being Honest

Body image and excess weight are my biblical *thorn in my side*. I am grateful for the help of all who know this disease. That help has brought me more sanity regarding my body and eating. Because struggle as I do, I did hear myself say on the phone yesterday that on a good day of healthy eating I am grateful for this disease, for it has brought me closer on my walk with God. Right now, fear is riding in the back seat of my car rather than driving me. I am most grateful for the grace to travel with it and not be driven by it.

My body image issue means that at times I see myself as fatter than I am. Sometimes the scale confirms this, but in other instances, I just don't like my body shape. This creates frustration when I am shopping for clothes.

I have this dream that when I get to a "perfect" size, shopping for clothes will be a breeze and a joy. My fantasy is walking into every store, choosing a few items, trying them on, and looking fabulous as I see my reflection in the mirrors. I did have that experience one time, and I believe that my mind goes to that memory and sets me up each time I shop. Typically, however, I am disappointed and frustrated. I have even commented to a friend how freeing it would be to have a private seamstress. Yes, it seems I have a princess mentality. What fun to dream! As I type this, I can see I need to smash that fantasy, for it truly is unrealistic. Woe is me!

You can see my struggle with weight in page after page in my journals, where I would be asking and begging God to help me lose weight. Many times this was after the delivery of each of my eight children.

One of my fears after giving birth to our eighth child was that my weight would escalate to a certain unacceptable number. The more I tried to control it, the worse it became.

I wasn't obese until my last pregnancy when I gained fifty pounds. I had postpartum depression, and this number filled me with fear. With the help of a church friend who dropped in one day, I came to acknowledge my depression and my fear of being out of control. That conversation, along with prayer, guided me to the library, where I found a book that led me to the help I needed with my out-of-control eating.

I came to see that I ate out of stress and to procrastinate. I would go to the kitchen and grab something to eat before I went downstairs to do the ironing that I didn't like doing. I also would go into the kitchen late at night while reading emotional novels. One of the big questions I had to ask myself was, "Am I staying up late to eat or eating to stay up late?" Even television commercials were another reason to run into the kitchen.

I remember shopping weekly at the discount bread store, buying coffee cakes for our Sunday breakfast, and always getting a second one. Once home, I would indulge, slice by slice, as I was putting the groceries away. I figured that if I ate it a little at a time, it wouldn't seem as bad!

I have an eating disorder that I have wrestled with for years. Sugar and white flour are my greatest temptations that lead me to lose control. One of something leads to two and more than is healthy for my body. Eating in the car, one energy bar at 3:30 p.m. leads to two and sometimes three. For a time I was buying a bag of what I call bullet caramel candies and gradually eating the whole bag on my way home from the store. I noticed I was going from store to store to feed my addiction. Prior to the candy, I was going to McDonald's for a soft-serve cone. For a while, when I went into Target, a certain dessert called to me. I couldn't wait to get home to eat it, of course, when no one else was around.

Another fear surrounding my eating behavior is what people will think of me when I am totally honest. My compulsive eating behavior embarrasses me, and there are several ways I act on this. One is to sneak eat. I will wait until our guests leave and my husband goes to bed. Then, there is the reluctance to write down a food plan for the day. This way I can kid myself by eating whatever I want whenever I want. I have come to identify my behavior as a rebellious spirit: doing what I want when I want.

Thankfully, it was suggested that I call my food into a friend. In doing this, I am making a commitment to another person as well as myself. It frees my mind from obsessive food thoughts.

Facing the Fear:

Honesty

Acknowledge:

Fear was freezing me. I badly needed help, which came to me in the gift of a therapist friend who just happened to drop in. She pointed out my depression that I was denying. I didn't want to think of myself as *that* weak. It was at this time that I was learning to walk through my emotions. While walking through my fear, I didn't realize the impact that action plays in overcoming fear.

Write:

I was daily taking time in prayer and began again to journal. This action helped to release my feelings. With the help of another therapist and nutritionist, I worked to take back control and slowly lose the pounds.

Did I mention I am a list maker? Recently I found a record of my weight from 1977, recorded every day for nine months. This obsession surprised me. I hadn't realized the intensity of my disease. I moved from daily weighing to weekly, to monthly, and then I threw out the scale. I began weighing myself monthly at the gym. That was a tremendous freedom.

Embrace:

Prayer, honesty, and action are the three behaviors that help me. I have come to see this eating issue as both a spiritual invitation and rebellion—the rebellion being doing what I want and not following the suggestions of recovered food addicts. A confidant suggested that I text a friend at night when I am tempted to eat. I cautiously began to do so. That has worked this past year for which I am most grateful, especially after years and years of nighttime eating. Thank you, God.

Fear of Trusting People

As an adult, after years of interrupted therapy, I got to the core of what I believe has distanced me from trusting people. During a therapy session, I remembered an incident that happened to me as a very young child. A trusted business employee who worked for my dad sexually violated me in our home. I expound on this in the "Fear of God" chapter.

This person, I was told later, displayed all the classic-predatory behaviors as he befriended me. I liked him. He kidded with me. He teased me. He showered a lot of attention on me, and then he abused me. After the abuse, he threatened that if I told anyone, the garbage men would take me away. After that, whenever I heard the garbage truck coming, I would run and hide in my closet. I had great fear of our refuse men. My parents never knew what happened. But that's not the only way this fear was born in me.

In my early teens, during the summer on Saturday morning, Dad would drive half an hour to the market and get half bushels of peaches, plums, pears, and tomatoes. We canned these foods. It was a tedious job that I vowed as a teen never to do when I got married and I haven't! During the school year, we each had to clean our rooms while listening to the radio program, *Let's Pretend*. It helped to pass the time. I did all the ironing, which included my dad's white starched shirts that he wore daily and cotton pants stretched on aluminum frames. Since we didn't have a dryer, socks and underwear also needed pressing. My next younger sister, Dolly, took care of Anne, our one-year-old baby sister, prior to our mom's death. Little did I realize Mom was guiding Dolly for a responsibility that Dolly dearly loved doing. I mention these tasks for it was mom's way of preparing us for her death.

Mom died in the month of February, when I was fourteen. There were highs and lows during her eighteen-month battle with ovarian cancer. One of the highs was mom dressed, coming downstairs for Mass on Christmas morning after having been bedridden for months. We all thought of it as a miracle. That was the last time we were all together. Our family included seventeen-year-old brother Bill, my sisters, Dolly (thirteen), Suzanne (eleven), Mary (eight), and Annie (one-and-a-half), plus me. Two months later, as mom was dying, she asked me if I would watch over and take care of my sisters. With tears, "Yes, of course," was my reply.

Along with that promise to my mother and her three years of prior guidance, I became very self-sufficient. I had an air of *can-do*. I grew up quickly. After the funeral, going back to school, the carefreeness that I watched my girlfriends exhibit was not mine to have. My friends were all solicitous and caring, but I felt different. I buried my pain again. I kept an emotional distance that I wasn't even aware of. I didn't want to get hurt again. How I acted, I don't know. All I do know is that I felt different. I felt more grown-up, but I did enjoy my high school years.

My grandmother (father's mother), who owned a four-family boarding home and lived three-hundred miles east, came to live with us for the first three months. I don't remember any conversation or memories spoken by my dad after Mom's death. One afternoon, while Gram was darning some socks in our dining room, she stated to me, "Jane, your mom lived a good life and now she has died and now we need to get on with life." I felt shocked. It sounded so cruel to me. I interpreted her comment as saying to me, "we won't talk about her anymore," and we didn't. Holding back tears, I ran up to my bedroom and sobbed.

Dad asked me to help clear out mom's dresser and closet. It was such an honor to do that. I loved her fashionable clothes. I kept and wore one of her dresses that included a long taffeta coat. I felt so grand and close to her.

During the summer after mom's death, Gram went back to her house. Our Dad and brother Bill went off to work while we girls were on our own with the meals and chores. What comes to mind is my *telling* my sisters what tasks to do, *not asking.* It was the beginning of my bossiness, being in charge with a controlling attitude that I have wrestled with most of my life. I realize my mom asked me to oversee the household, but it is my harshness or unloving demeanor that I regret.

Facing the Fear:
Trusting Others

Acknowledge:
I was and still am afraid of being hurt again. Innocence was taken from me not once, but twice, as a child. My anger and rage were buried and took years to process.

My husband, Don and I went on a marriage encounter weekend in 1974. That was the beginning of my learning about and acknowledging my feelings. I truly had no clue that there was a difference between thoughts and feelings. In my family growing up, feelings were not talked about that I remember. When I turned fifty, I began therapy. With the help of the fourth intermittent therapist, while talking about various issues, my anger about the death of my mother dying finally began to surface. I also got in touch with my anger at God for not performing the miracle of Mom living that we had prayed for.

This latent memory, guided and listened to by a most compassionate and wise woman, helped me to begin my healing and to begin to trust others. I share this, for it is a healing experience of walking through fear.

Today when other lesser fears raise their heads, I will name the situation, sit in prayer and begin working through the issue, and eventually embrace the fear. It takes time and prayer though for me. Sometimes I write a dialogue with the particular fear. I have also sat in silence, paying attention to where in my body I am holding the fear, what color it is, and what intensity. Tears are generally part of this process for me.

They show me my vulnerability. Over time I have noticed the lessening of that particular fear.

When I fight and deny the fear, I have come to see how it keeps resurrecting and becomes only stronger, wanting my attention. I have noticed that fear is a part of me that wants attention, just like joy or any other feeling. All this awareness has taken me years and years of processing for which I am now most grateful.

Write:

I am most grateful for all the writing processes people have shared with me over the years, such as the *Anger (feelings) Questions*. Writing, listening to people, praying, and taking action are my tools for living a more carefree life. These behaviors have helped me to become more trusting.

Embrace:

I am impressed with the following reading from Nelson Mandela. By working to accept this concept, I come closer to trusting myself and others.

"Our deepest fear is not that we are inadequate. Our deepest fear is that we are powerful beyond measure. It is our light, not our darkness, that most frightens us.

We ask ourselves, "Who am I to be brilliant, talented, gorgeous, fabulous? Actually, who are you not to be? You are a child of God: your playing small does not serve the world. There is nothing enlightened about shrinking so others will not feel insecure around you. We are born to make manifest the glory of God that is within us. It is not just in some of us; it is in every one of us. When we let our light shine, we unconsciously give others permission to do the same. As we are liberated from our deepest fears, so by our presence we liberate others."

-1994 Nelson Mandela inauguration speech.

Fear of Tight Spaces
(Claustrophobia)

When I think about this fear, the first memory is of my trip to Rome and the need to climb over three-hundred circular steps in the cupola of the Dome of St. Peter's Basilica in order to have a view of the Vatican grounds. The stairs are only one person wide and you can't turn around to come back down. You have to go to the top and then down another route. I didn't know this as I began my ascent.

We were ten or so steps up when I began to panic. I paused and looked around. There were people behind me as well as before me. It was most crowded. I wanted to get out of there. I felt panicky. I saw there was no way out and had to literally pray my way up the whole-heart pounding experience. Step by step, *Hail Mary*, step by step, *Full of Grace*; praying three-hundred steps to the roof level! I had never been so happy to be at the top of anything as I was to feel the wide-open space and fresh air. What a prayerful, scary experience it was.

Another experience years ago of one of my first times going into a cave scared me. It was dark and confining. I wasn't aware I had this condition. In the years since, I have thoroughly questioned the guides regarding unexplored caves and what the area is like, and I have passed up some cave excursions after hearing how confining it is. Others I will do. As long as I have open space around me, I am generally at peace.

If I am in a tightly packed elevator, my heart starts beating faster. My fear is of being confined and smothered. I am not aware of any childhood situations that led to this behavior. I do know I have gotten nervous when our children were playing with pillows and put them over each other's faces. What mother wouldn't?

An awareness that I am wondering might be tied in with this condition is selecting a table in a restaurant. I will choose a seat with my back to the wall so that I can look out upon the room. I don't know where this comes from, but I think it might be tied in with the claustrophobia. I also will look around the room to see where the exit is. Is this known as fear of being trapped? I don't know.

Facing the Fear:

Claustrophobia

Acknowledge:

I didn't realize I might be claustrophobic until I panicked in a cave. Since then I have noticed other situations that can evoke a fear response. So now, when I go on new adventures, I ask questions before entering an unknown environment. What are the conditions of the places I am going into, especially caves. The larger they are, especially with high ceilings, the more tolerable they seem to be for me. I have noticed many times when I go into a new place I look around for the exit. I want to know where to go if I begin to feel closed in.

Write:

As a result of my earlier writings, I have learned to take better care of myself. If my husband suggests visiting a new cave, I will ask the guide various questions such as how large it is, what the height of the ceiling is, is it well lit, and how confining the walkway is. This information helps me to be more informed and comfortable.

Embrace:

We can make many choices about our surroundings and situations. But there may still be circumstances when I feel this fear. All I know is that every time it happened to me, I was led to prayer to quiet my fear. I am grateful for that reprieve. I also try deep breathing.

Deep breathing and prayer are the two behaviors that help me relax and become open to the new experience.

Fear of Getting Lost

God created me as a directionally challenged person. It is only since I have finally begun to be open about how easily I get lost that I hear the same thing from other people. My favorite example is mentioning how I need to be purposeful before going into a revolving door by myself at a restaurant or building. I now will stop and look to see which way I want to go when I leave the building. I do this even before I go inside.

Prior to learning this intentional behavior, I would almost always exit the wrong direction to either my car or public transportation. And it would take me time to realize none of the environment looked familiar. I would panic and beat myself up emotionally by saying how dumb I was. For whatever reason, this occurred most of the time only after I had gone through a revolving door. I felt frustrated and panicky. This has been a weakness that humbles me and also helps me to be more attentive to my surroundings.

Driving alone into a big city like Chicago is also scary for me. The impatience of drivers, the congestion, and the unknown buildings and streets panic me and have kept me from venturing out on my own for years. Even in a new neighborhood, it is difficult for me to stop and ask for help. Pride!

As I was telling our older daughter, the other day that I was writing this chapter about fear of getting lost, she asked me if I wrote about the time I was with my dad and we got lost. I was twelve years old with the map on my lap, and Dad, who had a great sense of direction, was driving in Washington

DC. We needed to cross a bridge. We did, but then ended up going the wrong way. Dad, in his quiet way, asked me to check the map. He turned the car around and came back to where we began. I again directed him to what I was seeing on the map. And again we ended up the wrong way. There was no way to pull over. For a third time, we ended up on that silly bridge, going the wrong way. Dad finally was able to stop, took the map, and shook his head, trying to figure out what the problem was. Three times we went over that bridge. I don't remember him yelling at me. I just felt dumb and frustrated that I couldn't help my dad. My daughter today suggested this might have been a core incident indicating my directional challenge. Possibly was. I hadn't thought of it in a long time.

In downtown Chicago, we no longer have any free parking spots. There is a credit card payment system with stations a half block away from your car, causing you to make sure you know the number of your spot. If there is no parking available nearby, I am forced to drive on and around the block, leading me to a one-way street. Being directionally challenged, I then get panicked after driving around several one-way streets, trying to figure out which way I need to go to find my original destination.

The hard part is that I love to drive, but congestion makes me uneasy. Having a GPS in my car certainly has brought me some comfort recently, but that too has at times taken me, should I say, *for a ride*. As I write this, I can also add aging to my fear and hesitation to drive alone downtown. I just don't do it.

I sound like a country girl, but I grew up in Cleveland where I was very comfortable driving in the city. This fear has been most humbling for me.

******

Yesterday, I had another opportunity to grow. Gary, one of our sons living out of state, was in town for a business interview. He decided to come a few days early to spend extra time with us. Don, my husband, who is a motivational speaker, had a seminar out of town that week. Having a free day, Gary asked me if I wanted to go downtown with him and hang out while he had an hour visit with Dave, his brother who works downtown.

My husband and I live in the suburbs, twenty-five miles west of Chicago. Gary mentioned we would have free time until 1:00 p.m. Two days earlier I had shared with Gary how Don and I would love to rent a place downtown for a month just to see what it would be like living there. Opportunist and thoughtful person that Gary is, he proposed this outing. Little did he know that I was hesitant because I felt scared. I rely on Don for our downtown trekking around, both getting there and once there, walking around. I thought Gary, having lived in Georgia for so many years, wasn't familiar with the streets and transportation, so the guidance would fall on me.

The day before I gave Gary my answer, I was talking to my friend, and she was encouraging me to go, to enjoy the special time alone with my son, and to overcome my fear. She also mentioned how we could work together getting around. Her enthusiasm was so contagious that I told her I would do it. When Gary got home, I told him I would go. He then said, "Mom, we will do whatever you want to do."

Oh no, I thought. I have to make a plan; I have to be responsible. To just walk around idly isn't acceptable to me. I need to have a destination. I went on the Internet and looked up free activities for Tuesday in Chicago. I was given all kinds of suggestions. Then I went downstairs and found a map and started marking the times and locations of the ideas. I was beginning to feel excited.

The next morning as we left, it began to sprinkle. I was getting cold feet but pulled on my courage boots and suggested we take umbrellas. We got to the Rapid Transit parking lot and the first automatic payment machine wouldn't accept my dollar. This prompted a memory.

I told Gary a story from months ago when Chicago first put in the new payment system and we had problems with our dollar bills. Don and I decided to risk not paying since it was Sunday. Don is a law-abiding person, so I was very surprised when I heard him say, "In the past on Sundays, they didn't care if you paid."
"Okay," I said, and off we went.

When we came home from our outing, we couldn't find our car. There weren't many cars in the lot, so it didn't take us long to make that discovery. We were nervous! I could feel my heart racing. Where was it? "No," we each said, as we looked at one another, "they didn't tow it?" Sure enough! Getting the car back is another story that I won't go into now. One-hundred and fifty dollars was our charge. That was a very expensive three-dollar fee that Don and I ignored on a Sunday.

Needless to say, I told Gary we had to figure out how to pay this fee. We went to the next machine twenty feet away, and that was out of order. I prayed for help and along came a car, driving past us to the third paying station. I went over to the woman driver and asked her for help. I gave her my dollars, and for whatever reason, that machine worked.

The next hurdle was Gary getting his train ticket. I had mine. Another automatic machine! People helped us. We didn't have four singles and the machine wouldn't give a dollar change from our five-dollar bill, so he got a one-way ticket and decided we would get change downtown at lunchtime and get the return ticket then. I don't like these machines. I feel dumb because I never need to use them and can't figure them out, but I am coming to see that usually there are people around to help. This is another area that I am recently being called to exercise... asking for help! Once again, God took care of us.

And what a fun time I had downtown! Gary and I experienced a one-hour tour of the Chicago Theatre for five dollars. We walked to one of my favorite places downtown, the Cultural Center, where we saw a puppet show in progress. We stayed there fifteen minutes and then I showed Gary around the gorgeous, historic building with Tiffany lighting and fabulous inlaid tiles, and we viewed two art exhibits.

We then walked to Dave's office and while the boys went for coffee, I went to the Loft women's store and found two skirts that were marked down twice. That made my day! I then met up with the boys; Gary and I grabbed a sandwich while Dave went back to work. On our train ride home, Gary and I were both commenting on how special it was for just the two of us to be together and what a fun time we each had. I am so glad that he asked me to come along and I am so grateful for these experiences that help me grow, even though these opportunities are uncomfortable. And did I tell you? It didn't rain!

Facing the Fear:
Getting Lost

Acknowledge:

To work through the revolving door fear of getting lost, I had to first recognize it, then name it, and accept it. Then I began to ask myself how I could embrace it. Journaling helped to bring the fear to the surface rather than hiding in the recesses of my mind. I began being more cognizant of my surroundings, especially when alone. It was hard. I swallowed my pride and asked people to confirm my directions before leaving a building. Each of my fears has been a growing experience.

Facing fear can be an opportunity for growth, like my fear of driving downtown alone at night into an unfamiliar area. It embarrassed me, but I told my husband and he graciously did a trial ride in the daylight with me for several days.

Only since I have been more open and honest with others have, I come to also see that I am not alone with this condition. It sure has been comforting.

Write:

"Thank you, my God, for all the coincidences and for opening me to notice the experiences." Through writing, I am aware of the ongoing healing of fear by driving to unfamiliar places by myself, and I am reminded how comfortable I recently felt driving to the courthouse in Chicago for jury duty.

Embrace:

The first time I drove to the courthouse may have been ten years ago. I was scared and nervous. This time I was comfortable. The building looked like it had been moved (it hadn't) and was in a safer setting. The people around me didn't even look as menacing. In the parking lot, rather than being uncomfortable, I was able to smile at others and ask for directions to the courthouse. That helped me feel more assertive and at ease with myself. I was given the courage to walk out of the building for lunch, even though I had the thought of staying in the jury holding room. I bought lunch from a vendor on the street. That was new behavior for me. I felt free to kid with people in the hall waiting for the elevator. It was a whole different experience.

Fear of Appearing Dumb

In addition to my directional handicap, for years I was not willing to ask for help when lost. I've lived with the attitude that I should know everything, and asking for help made me feel dumb. Stopping at a gas station asking where the restaurant was, I would hear the attendant say, "Go east three blocks, turn right and then go blah, blah, blah." My mind would blank out with the fear rising of getting lost. I am grateful for the GPS that I use a lot now. Yes, it has misdirected me at times, but eventually, I get to my destination.

When my husband and I traveled before the GPS, if we were lost, he would be the one to stop and ask for help. Some of the few times that I had asked, I would come out and in retelling, it didn't make sense. A few times I asked the attendant to write it down. Of course, the greatest experience was when the person said, "Oh, it's just a block down the road."

One entertaining story using the GPS was when I was driving by myself from Chicago to Cleveland a few years ago. In the address setup, I reversed the street and suburb names. As I came into downtown Cleveland, I encountered major construction in an area I used to be very familiar with. My GPS took me on a main road that looked different to me. I drove it for a while and then came to a detour that took me to a more unfamiliar territory. Around and around I drove, three times. The roads were all torn up; it was residential with no one around. I couldn't even pull over because of the construction. While praying, I finally took a different road that eventually delivered me to the area I wanted. I had been circling for an hour and was so frustrated. I couldn't figure out what had happened.

Relief enveloped me as I pulled up to my brother's house. I still felt frustrated, arrived later than I had anticipated, and couldn't figure out the issue. I didn't understand what happened until I went over the directions with my brother, who kindly pointed out my mix-up. I looked again at my GPS in disbelief and shook my head. I couldn't believe how I had transposed the address and suburb name. Laughter relieved the horrible tension I felt. Thank goodness I have a good sense of humor, although it took me some time to become peaceful.

Another experience of appearing dumb was when I was a teenager. Dad was driving us to his business. I was talking to him about something. I don't remember what it was. All I remember is his saying, "Jane, think before you speak." His admonishment shot right into my heart.

My father was a gentle spirit. I don't remember him ever correcting me about anything, so this wounded me like an arrow. I have no idea why he said that, other than thinking he wasn't able to follow my babbling. Was I making a statement he didn't agree with? I have no idea. I do know that his words had a paralyzing effect on me.

In a group, when a speaker asks if there are any questions, or asks for feedback, I am hesitant to raise my hand, feeling self-conscious. I have come to notice this over and over again. I usually have an opinion or question but remain silent. I say to myself that I will talk with him/her later, one on one if I get the chance. "Jane, think before you speak."

Facing the Fear:

Appearing Dumb

Acknowledge:

I have accepted that I am directionally challenged. I don't want to compound it by feeling dumb, so I have learned to work with it by using the GPS and double-checking the address. Sometimes I will even print out directions before I leave or I write them down myself.

Write:

Today, as I am writing and thinking about my dad's statement, "Jane, think before you speak," I am challenged to use the *Anger (feelings) Questions* I have been taught. I feel directed to share them with you as an example right now, unedited. I use them over and over again for clarity in my life. You can find them printed below.

Embrace:

The greatest gift is learning to accept myself as God created me and looking at my handicaps with a sense of humor rather than hesitating to take action out of fear, as was my past behavior.

Example from my journaling:

ANGER (feelings) QUESTIONS

- What makes me angry?
  That dad couldn't follow my stories.
- What is the real issue?
  Not speaking freely
- What do I think and feel?
  Hurt, I felt hurt, so I kept quiet. I think I might have been babbling and he couldn't follow my story. I feel sad thinking I internalized his admonishment.
- What do I want to accomplish?
  I want to forgive him and myself and begin to be freed up to be myself.
- Who is responsible for what?
  I am responsible for forgiving both of us him for his statement and me for resenting it. (tears as I write)
- What do I want to change?
  I want to feel freedom to speak up at appropriate times after considering my words.
- What are the things I will and will not do?
  I will forgive us both, me for resentment and him for not being perfect. *Thank you, God.*

(I did not answer the *will not do* part of this question this time.)

I felt enlightened and freed up after this writing as usually happens to me. These questions are a great tool.

Fear of My Husband Dying First

Finances

Another fear that lies below the surface of my living carefree is thinking periodically of Don, my husband, dying before me. This fear has several aspects to it. The first one that comes to mind is managing our finances.

When we were first married our income management was quite simple. I was a stay-at-home mom, so we only had Don's income. We decided I could and would manage our money. We lived in Ft. Benning, Georgia where the Army paid Don once a month. At the beginning of the month, I would write out checks for church and our bills. I loved knowing our expenses were covered at the beginning of the month. I also had three envelopes of cash that I carried around in my purse: one for food, one for clothing, and one for gas and entertainment.

The first six months, we kept track of our expenses. This gave us the knowledge we needed for our envelopes. There were times toward the end of the month when I needed extra food money or some apparel, so I "borrowed" from entertainment. My point is I was liberal with this system and used the money as was needed. I relished knowing how our money was being spent. I didn't realize then that I have a control issue, and this system was one way of me knowing where our money was being spent.

Years later, in civilian life, I was busy raising our eight children and Don took over disbursing our money. Don was being paid weekly. He put the money into a checking account and paid all the bills. I would write a check for whatever I needed, including cash for groceries. This system worked well until Don went to night school.

As the children grew older and new expenses arose, we decided to budget *together,* talking about the upcoming needs. This process worked for a number of years until Don began investing and working with a financial planner. We went to meetings together where we were educated with a different approach to handling our money. Don was in banking, comfortable and knowledgeable regarding money. I had a difficult time understanding various concepts. It was like going from high school to graduate school. The language felt foreign to me, and I didn't want any part of it. So Don once again took over managing our coins and has done a fabulous job. What a relief it was for me.

However, as some of my friends have lost their spouses, I hear their stories of needing to be more self-reliant. I am aware of how inept I am in this area. Don has always encouraged me to come with him to the financial seminars, and I have at times. He also mentions how our children will be there to help me should he die first. It is a trust issue for me in an area where I am not comfortable.

Facing the Fear:
Handling the Finances

Acknowledge:
Hearing of the struggle some of my friends have had to face when their husbands died has brought this fear to the surface. Don and I have kidded with each other saying, "I hope you don't die first because…" and we go on talking about our inadequacies, mine being financially savvy.

We have talked about our financial planners and our children as resources who would be helpful if this fear comes to fruition. We have talked with several of our sons who have agreed to oversee our finances if need be, so I do have help at my disposal. What I am aware of though, is what a financial student Don has become in this area and how stylized our portfolio is. Of course, I am thinking from a protective attitude that no one would manage our money the same way.

Write:
I have written many times on this fear and know that there are still feelings I need to address. Writing has shown me that this fear can be another opportunity for me to ask for help, which I have previously mentioned is hard for me. I do have to admit some of this fear walks side by side with my friend, *control*, another big area in my life that I am continually wrestling with.

Embrace:
So I continually pray, go to a few seminars, talk with a planner periodically, and pray again that God will protect and guide me.

Surrender, over and over again, is my action and prayer. I believe these fears have been an indirect gift from God, leading me to growth in prayer, acceptance, and reliance on this available power.

P.S. I did tell you that Don is a most loving, considerate, and kind man and a great steward of our money

Filing Cabinets

Another fear that haunts me is of Don, my husband of fifty-nine years, dying first and my having to go through the five, four-drawer filing cabinets where he has stored his desired paperwork including utility receipts, credit card offers, banking files, investment reports, health care info, and some general articles that he wants to keep. The good news is that they all are in cabinets. The bad news is that it is overwhelming to me. There is so much to go through. Every so often I get a bee in my bonnet and want Don to get rid of stuff. This usually happens when I am bored or don't have a project of my own. I then get into Don's business. He has been most loving putting up with my controlling nature all these years.

For the most part, I am not a saver. I do have my paints and art collection, along with a cabinet of retreat folders that I am beginning to recycle. I also have books and three boxes of journals. None of these items are important to anyone else.

I am not a sentimental person. Don is. He loves taking pictures. We had seventeen year's worth of slides stored that needed (according to me) to be edited. Together, five years ago we began that process.

He has articles of people and family members that seem important to him. He was in marketing for many years. He would receive brochures and ideas on paper that he thought would be helpful. They got filed. "Someday I may need these," he would say. He is an excellent motivational speaker who has stored ten years of prep work. All of these cabinets are full.

My fear is of throwing out material that might be important. Some would say just toss it all. But if I don't go through it, I may get rid of needed documents for the estate. Also, there is anger that I will have to be the one to do all this purging of papers I wouldn't have kept.

Facing the Fear:

My Husband Dying First (file cabinets, paper accumulation, and sides.)

Acknowledge:

One awareness I have had is that when **I** am procrastinating and not doing what I need to do with my business and activities, I will then focus on Don's territory or as some say, "get on his case." Also, I don't like the thought of being left alone and forced to clean up his stuff.

Write:

We have been fortunate to travel to many countries. At times now I will stop myself from nagging Don about all the bags of travel brochures he treasures. Feeling frustrated I ask myself in my writing, "What am *I* procrastinating about?" Most of the time my words point out something I have been avoiding. This has been a helpful realization and has taken many, many years to develop. In the past, it was easier for me to be critical of him than to face my own demons.

Embrace:

Regarding the slides, Don and I recently reviewed seventeen years of picture slides. Five years ago we got rid of all the scenery ones and presently are going through the people slides, saving those dear to both of us. Don will have them scanned and put in the cloud. Then we will be rid of one-hundred and seventy-eight boxes and left with wonderful memories we can review by computer. As of this writing, I am so happy to report that Don is almost finished scanning all of them. It has been several months of daily visits to our library. He has been so diligent. Yes, I do have a wonderful husband and am so grateful to have a thoughtful, family-loving husband. I also realize these issues are about me and my intolerance. I just keep working on my defects. Acceptance happens along with action.

Fear of The Unknown

Writing

I have journaled for years and enjoy the freedom and insights that come with putting my thoughts and feelings down on paper. When I was in my late forties, I wrote in my journal about the desire of writing a book but didn't have any idea what to write. This prompt kept showing up in my journals over and over again for the next six years until I went to a workshop for blocked artists. The workshop was called *The Artist's Way*.

A month into the twelve-week workshop, I went into town for a meeting in the back of a store. Yvonne Petterson, a woman and former business editor who none of us knew, walked into our gathering unexpectedly. After she introduced herself to the group, I quickly introduced myself and asked if she would be interested in working with me while I wrote a book. She suggested we meet and have some conversation to see if we were a fit. A week later, our journey together began. After reading some of my writings, she suggested I had three books, and that I had to decide which one to focus on. Her discernment was priceless. I will forever be grateful to her for her selfless giving of time and insights. I chose to focus on my autobiography, **Seasons of My Heart, Life Is a Struggle but the Payoff is Worth It.**

Initially, the fear was of the unknown. I didn't know how to proceed with writing a book. Where do I start? How do I start? I didn't know what to write about and I didn't have anyone to guide me. Those previous six years were truly an internal agony. I kept getting the nudges in prayer and in my journaling to write a book.

I was begging God to guide me, but nothing happened until I took the first step and went to that twelve-week workshop. Then I also received the amazing awareness that ninety-five men and women of all different artistic endeavors were also blocked in their crafts. It was most comforting to know that I wasn't alone.

Week after week we gathered to do exercises that challenged our excuses and gave us the courage to move along. What a gift.

Three years later, after finishing my autobiography, Yvonne suggested I write a fiction book. Again I felt so uncertain, actually paralyzed. A month later, I began an ABC book for toddlers. I wanted to overcome my fear of writing fiction and my resistance to change from non-fiction to fiction.

Several weeks later, I went to the bookstore to see what was already on the shelf. After I thumbed through the variety of little tykes' books, I left, feeling deflated, thinking what I had written wasn't good enough and different enough, so I put those twenty-seven pages in a file folder where they remain today. Maybe someday I will resurrect them, or maybe one of my grandchildren will find my attempt and restructure it. Doesn't hurt to have some wishful thinking. Actually, it takes me off the hook. I continued to journal but felt shut down with my creative words. A number of years have passed and here I am with this fear book after again being guided to write non-fiction.

I wanted to believe Yvonne but just couldn't bring myself to write a fiction book. I don't see myself as a fiction writer. That may be my first problem. I cannot visualize the make-believe world. I am a facts person. I love to read mostly nonfiction, and I love to hear about people's lives.

As I thought about writing this book about my fears, I kept arguing with myself, denying that I am a fearful person. "Not me! I won't have much to say on this topic," I reasoned. Obviously, my thinking has proven faulty, much to my chagrin.

Day by day, week by week, as I was talking with people about their fears, I began to identify with them. Wow! I couldn't believe it. Then I found an old workbook that I had filled in and was faced with a few more fears. From that book, I read one of my current twelve-step books and found a chapter on fears. I began to honestly admit that I had more fears. That was the catalyst for me to begin writing this book. As I identified one fear, I came to see another. These collective fears surprised me. "Okay, I guess I have enough material for a book on fears," I reasoned.

After lamenting one day to a friend about identifying these fears, she jested, "Welcome to the human race, Jane."

Sure is wonderful having lighthearted friends.

Facing the Fear:

Writing

Acknowledge:

I needed to take action to overcome my fear but didn't know what action to take. I just kept journaling. Little did I realize that my daily writings were material that I would use. It seems my daily journaling was the action until the *Artist's Way* opportunity. I didn't realize how God was guiding me.

Write:

I went to the *Artist's Way* workshop at night, for twelve weeks, a forty-five-minute drive from home. I knew no one but had the strong sense to go. The cost was a big decision too because, at the time, we had no extra dollars. By writing about my indecision, the idea of using my squirreled away inheritance money surfaced. I didn't go to college and thought this would be a great way to honor myself. It was a wonderful investment that began my book-writing career.

Embrace:

Writing, writing, and more writing has been the catalyst to help me see my fear of writing a book. Talking with an introspective friend also helped me to name this fear. Prayer and the action of going to the course and hearing so many other people being afraid of their artistry was what I needed to realize I wasn't alone with my fear.

Marketing My Book

Another fear of the unknown realm was the marketing of my books and art. The publishing and marketing business were so foreign to me that it froze me. I felt stymied, paralyzed to even begin researching what to do. I had no idea where to even begin. After talking with several trusted people, I took a first step.

After I wrote my autobiography, **Seasons of My Heart,** I went to the library to find books of publishing companies. A few weeks later, I sent out thirteen query letters to publishers. I didn't get picked up. I didn't have an agent either. I did have an editor though, who was most helpful with my writing, and I am forever grateful for her gracious time and insights.

After waiting impatiently, I decided to self-publish. In prayer, I had the sense this was the way I was to proceed. After talking with several printing companies and selecting one, I made decisions regarding the cover, the color, and the picture, plus the size of the book. I ordered one thousand copies figuring that to be the best price.

My objective was to cover my investment cost by speaking and selling as many books as I needed. I called libraries, contacted friends and churches to let them know I was available to speak about my book. It was and is most fearful for me to promote myself (fear of rejection), but I knew that there was a purpose in writing my book and I was compelled to get it into circulation.

I am proud to say I accomplished my goal. However, I do have some books left in boxes in my front closet. And my fear continued after reaching my goal. I didn't want to make myself vulnerable any more than I needed. I am most grateful for having followed through with the writing for three years and for having given the presentations. Heaven only knows how the remaining books will be distributed.

Facing the Fear:
Marketing

Acknowledge:

Fear to me is a motivator, though I don't like the feeling. I don't like sitting with the discomfort. An awareness I have had is that the sooner I acknowledge I am fearful, the easier it is to walk through it. When I admitted this fear to several friends, my resistance melted, and I took action.

Write:

I have noticed with all my feelings that when I name and write about them, they aren't as powerful. They lose some of their intensity. Rather than inhibit me, the emotions then walk side by side with me. It has taken me years to learn this important lesson. I need to be willing to act. I journaled for many weeks about this fear of not knowing what to do. I also thought about all the time I had put into writing my book. Finally, I got sick and tired of my inaction.

Embrace:

I learned it is only by embracing my fear and walking through it that I can then be free. When I went to the library, I took the first step to embrace this fear of the unknown.

Fear of Not Being Good Enough

I was in my fifties and feeling restless. The children were all in school and I was wondering what I was going to do with the rest of my life. I noticed an invitation to attend a retreat using watercolors as a medium for expressing oneself. I love going on a yearly retreat. It is an important time for me to be quiet and introspective, wondering what God has in mind to tell me.

The ad mentioned that no prior art experience was needed. That's good because I never took any art classes. I do remember that in kindergarten I colored a robin. I loved putting a red-orange breast on the image. That was the extent of art for me.

The retreat invitation stated the weekend would be an opportunity to express our inner yearnings in a safe and encouraging environment. It was being held at a location close to my house. That was unusual and sounded wonderful. I made a reservation for the weekend.

The art teacher had a soft, calming voice and gave clear directions as we twelve women sat listening to her. She mentioned we would be painting in silence for ninety minutes each time, several times a day. We were to pay attention to our inner voice and feelings during the time we expressed ourselves on watercolor paper. We were to try to let go of any intentional painting, to let the colors choose us, and then let our brush guide the paints. We were encouraged to journal if we cared to. I became aware of inner stirrings. I took several breaks, looking at what I had painted in an abstract way. I wanted to be in touch with my body.

I looked around the room a number of times and began to feel inadequate as I noticed some paintings that looked professionally done. I thought, "I am not good enough to be with this group." I questioned myself, wondering what I had gotten myself into, although there were a few paintings that looked as amateurish as mine. I knew not to compare, but human nature is what it is. I loved the silence. It gave me time to be attentive to what I was doing, although at times that was an issue for me.

I do most things fast. I drive fast, I walk fast, I work fast, and I painted fast. I had three paintings finished while the other ladies were still on their first. After several painting sessions, the instructor suggested we then be intentional with our creativity. For me, it was painstaking to slow down. I didn't like it at all. It felt like someone had handcuffed my wrists.

On the second day of the weekend, after cleaning up our paints, we sat in a circle and were asked to share the awareness we might have had while painting. This encouraged some ladies to show their art and explain their insights. I saw such varied expressions, mostly professional-looking which caused me to be hesitant to show my work. I had three times as many sheets and judged my art as poorly expressed. I felt insecure.

At the end of our time, we were invited to not show our works but share with the group what we became aware of during the painting time. I loved hearing from the women the different insights they had while painting. We were encouraged strongly *not to* compare our work with others and to trust the process, letting the paintings speak for themselves. I don't remember my response but do remember looking around and comparing my work with others while painting.

Since I enjoyed the weekend, I decided to participate in the upcoming monthly experience. I painted with the group for twenty years until our creative space was moved to another building where I didn't feel comfortable. Also, having three hundred plus paintings in my closet gave me the incentive to stop. I haven't figured out how to get rid of them yet.

With the help of my daughter-in-law, I did create two art books pairing my poems with an appropriate painting. I thought this was a way to honor my works. I have cut up a few paintings and made greeting cards. Several I cut into bookmark strips, laminated, and gave away as gifts. Seems like there is always a creative challenge around my corner.

I am surprised, when I look back, at the endeavors I've said yes to. It probably is good that I don't know what lies ahead. I most likely would say no, like a two-year-old, out of fear. All I know is, I am grateful once again to my God for leading me to these new experiences and my being willing to try them.

Facing the Fear:

Not Being Good Enough

Acknowledge:

The weekend was a prerequisite if I wanted to attend future monthly, two-hour painting sessions with about ten ladies. I still had the fear of not being good enough, but the group setting was encouraging. Since I loved painting in silence and there was no critiquing, I felt accepted by the women. I also felt supported to accept my own style of painting, and I wanted to continue.

Write:

We began our monthly sessions in a circle, singing a little song of release. Having selected and paid for our paper, we hung it on the wallboards and set up our supplies on a long table in a spacious area. Monthly we brought our own paints and brushes, filled the water containers, and silently began watercolor and eventually tempura painting while standing.

I often stopped to check in with myself, asking what color wanted to be expressed, and then began in silence with the other ladies. After completing one piece I would pick up my pen and record what I was seeing and feeling. I loved the times I saw humor in my art and journaled about it. The journaling helped me see more than my inadequacy. I loved the process.

Embrace:

I continually faced my demons and began learning things about myself.

- I realized how fast I work and asked myself if it is okay to slow down. I never learned that lesson and decided it was okay.
- Is it okay not to have a skilled talent? I did finally accept that.
- Don't compare myself with others. I had to continually remind myself.
- Can I have fun just expressing myself in a carefree, not planned manner? Little by little I began to play and enjoy some of my works, and after encouragement, had several framed.

I wrestled with the desire of wanting to be noticed for many months until I finally came to grips with the realization that I wasn't creating to exhibit but to express my inner emotions. The reminder quieted my fear of rejection and of "not being good enough."

Once I accepted the fact that I was expressing my emotions, I began to relax and have fun, even finding humor in some of my art pieces. The fear of criticism that never came and the acceptance of not being perfect gradually grew.

I finally began to see that I have my own style, and every so often I noticed a painting of mine that I liked. From my perspective, I decided it was worthy of framing and that is all that matters. I am grateful for the insights I received monthly. Finally, I came to feel joy as I gazed upon some of my paintings.

Fear of Losing My Faith

Early in my walk with God, I became aware of going down the wrong spiritual path. I was afraid that I would follow a walk that took me to an evil place, a place away from God, a place of darkness, and that I would end up in a black hole. Where this came from I have no idea.

I know that many fears are irrational, (**F**alse **E**vidence **A**ppearing **R**eal), but nonetheless, they can quietly sneak into my psyche.

Years ago while I was on a retreat, a lady friend came up to me during break and asked me to be her spiritual director. I felt honored but scared and said, "No, I can't. I don't have any training."

I felt bad turning her down for I knew how I loved my own spiritual director. I look forward to visiting with my spiritual director each month, knowing I will have an hour with someone who listens to my life's journey, concerns, and moments of grace. Little did I realize that this lady was a beautiful gift to me, planting the seed for me to consider future training as a Spiritual Director.

Two years later, after seeing an ad in our Catholic paper for Spiritual Director's training, I felt an inner nudge, prayed, and asked for God's guidance.

Soon after, I met with my confessor and also my spiritual director, explained about the opportunity, and asked their advice. I received both of their recommendations and prayers.

But now, to take the training, another fear: driving into Chicago at night. I have talked about how easily I get lost. This training experience was scheduled before GPS was available and would be a nighttime drive to a new area. I knew deep within this was the journey I was to take. I was excited about it. My husband, Don, encouraged me to sign up, and I had the support of two other trusted people.

The Spiritual Direction training was sponsored by our archdiocese and led by two theologically trained women. One I knew personally and respected.

The second week in one of our sessions, I heard information from them about a bible story that was contrary to my childhood upbringing. I could feel the beginning of my racing heart. I read the bible daily and sometimes questioned the readings, but to hear something contrary from learned ladies scared me. This seemed huge.

At this point in my life, I was a black-and-white thinking person. There was no room for gray. And here I was being led to think differently and was scared. One leader mentioned how some held beliefs were not true as worded but were written in allegory. "Wait a minute," I thought. This threatened the core of beliefs that I had held for forty years. I felt scared. It was like the rug was being pulled out from under my feet and I was landing on my butt, hitting my head and shaking my thinking.

It took several conversations with the leader, a talk with my spiritual advisor, and months more before I became comfortable with this new concept. I was being cracked open to entertain gray in my life. Before this moment, there was no room for other ways of looking at things. It was the beginning of possibility thinking, not black or white. Even today, my spiritual director sometimes corrects me and suggests I slip in the word "and." She will ask me, "Jane, could it be this *and* that?"

I had to shed my childhood learning and begin my adult ownership of beliefs. It was uncomfortable and quite threatening to leave the comfort of my parents' teachings.

Today, I can accept differences that I refused to entertain years ago. Much of this freedom has been due to prayer, conversations, seminars, writing, and guidance from the spiritual director who has mentored me for over twenty years. As a matter of fact, I have two women who have walked with me for years. I am so blessed with the people God has put in my path.

******

One morning, as I was writing, I had a lot of tears with the thought of losing my faith. I felt deep emotion thinking of not having God in my life. And then a few months later a priest I respect asked at Mass if we wanted to get to know Jesus more. To myself, I said "no" and continued, "I already know Him and love Him and have a comfortable relationship."

I was bothered throughout the day with a nagging discomfort regarding my answer. After taking several days in prayer and writing, I called the priest and had a conversation with him. He only knew me from attendance at weekly Mass, so it was a big step for me to be vulnerable and open with him.

The priest said, "to really love someone, one needs to fully know Him." I felt a little better after our talk but continued to feel unsettled. I felt arrogant with my thinking. I acted out with my compulsive overeating for several days afterward, wondering what was going on. It wasn't until I took more time to journal that I discovered I was using my food addiction to cover up my feelings.

I spent days in prayer asking for God's clarity. I was sorry for my defiance and sorry for shutting the door on God's love that continually is available when I am open to receive it. I also told God that I realized I hadn't given Him a chance to *show off* His love when I had shut down by overeating. This pearl and thorn in my side of addiction have brought me much awareness in life.

During prayer days later, I surrendered myself once again into God's hands, feeling trepidation. I ended with a prayer: *Into Your Hands I commit my spirit O Lord. Amen.*

The next morning I came downstairs to write about my fear of God. I found through my written word, it was more my fear of losing God in my life. I like to write with classical music playing in the background. Many times I will choose Beethoven or Bach. That day I chose piano music and as I was writing, tears welled up. What came to me was the love I had for my dad's gift of playing the piano. I loved listening to the beautiful way his fingers rolled across the keys. At night, Dad would play selections for us six children as we went to sleep. Many times if he stopped, I yelled down to him to play some more. It is a touching memory for me to remember his gentle spirit and piano-playing gift.

As I wrote that day, the memory of my dad's love and God's love seemed to be the same. I thought of how often I take it for granted, just as I did with my dad's unconditional love expressed especially in his piano playing at night, a lullaby of sorts.

Taking life for granted, taking people for granted, and not realizing the fullness of their gifts while they were alive, led me to discover too late how my father loved me. My father died many years ago, but today, writing about my heavenly Father's love, I have an opportunity to embrace God's gifts. *Thank you, Abba today for revealing Your love to me, again.*

I remember seven years ago compiling my underlined Bible verses and noticing they all had to do with forgiveness. Here I am once more with tears, this time, tears of sadness and remorse for not recognizing the unconditional love God has for me. Forgive me, God, for turning my back on Your open arms. I know I can't earn Your love, though I can be open to ways You want to help me live my life with more serenity and peace.

I want to be open to all the ways You love me, including through my dad's piano playing.

Facing the Fear:
Losing My Faith

Acknowledge:

I want to reinforce the importance of prayer and talking through concerns with a trusted person. I was scared. I questioned God in prayer, wondering why He was guiding me to this new awareness. Little did I realize how I needed to be cracked open. Along with the people He put in my path, and my willingness to be open, His grace sustained me.

As a child, I heard over and over again how my Catholic religion was the one, true religion. You can imagine my surprise when years later at several meetings I heard ladies share how they were raised with the same belief of *their* Baptist or Presbyterian religion. I gulped when I first heard that and then laughed to myself thinking how many of us are walking around with these narrow beliefs.

Write:

It is freeing for me to believe that God is bigger than our religions. Today my truth is that *God is Mystery*. I believe He/She loves everyone and if we are so different does that mean He/She loves us conditionally? I don't believe that.

It certainly has taken a lot of years writing and life experiences to let go of my preconceived ideas and open myself to the Spirit's guidance in trusting that God has my best interest in His/Her hand.

Embrace:

After holding the fear of driving alone to downtown Chicago at night up to the light, talking to a friend and admitting how scared I was, she suggested picturing Jesus in the passenger seat next to me keeping me company. The nights I was to drive into the city, I put on my seat belt and did imagine Jesus sitting there in the passenger seat next to me. I said a prayer with Him and off we went. Hard as it was, another gift was the opportunity to drive six weeks in a row into the city, which helped me to overcome this fear. It finally gave me a feeling of confidence that I continue to experience.

Trust. Over and over again! That is a word I want to embrace more and more. The opposite of fear is trust. Trust I will be taken care of. Trust that God wants only good for me. It is I who may take the wrong path, and I am trusting God will be there at the end of the road with open arms to love me.

Fear of God

I had a fear that God was judging me. I was raised with the attitude of a harsh God. I thought my God was hovering, waiting to see me make a mistake, and He would then mark down an *x* in my *diary of life*. I never thought of God the Father as loving, which is strange because I had a very easygoing, gentle father. My fear belief came from my school and church training that God was watching everything I was doing, and so I had better behave. I interpreted His watchfulness negatively. I believe I was an obedient child, though as a toddler I created excitement and maybe a little mischief!

I am told that when I was two years old a neighbor called my mom, telling her I was sitting on the second-floor open window ledge with my legs dangling, looking out at the world. I also locked myself in the second-floor bathroom. My mom had to call the fire department to get me out. Another incident spoken about is one afternoon when I was three years old, I climbed up on the top of our console piano, entertainingly singing, and my mom was jolted out of her reverie.

At five years old, after telling mom I was running away, she hugged me and said goodbye, thinking I would just go on our front porch. A while later, a neighbor friend called and said "Greta, I just want to let you know Janie's here." I was two blocks down the street with my little suitcase. My poor mom had her hands full with me, I guess. Doesn't seem like I had many fears then, just adventure.

I was raised as a Roman Catholic and experienced my first sacraments of Confession and Communion as a seven-year-old. I had twelve years of Catholic school instruction incorporating the Ten Commandments. Our training with loving Ursuline sisters was of a demanding and harsh God. I was taught we are to love, honor, and obey God. For the most part, I did exercise these three words; however, **obey** seemed to be a challenging word.

In turning fifty, I began to test the waters again like a two-year-old. I acted out in little ways that were fun and big for me. I chuckle as I write this: I would safely drive *into the exits* and *out the entrances*. I rebelled in small ways.

In the Catholic tradition, we believe in the Trinity: God the Father, Jesus, and the Holy Spirit. I realize now that I needed a healing with God the Father from suppressed memories of abuse inflicted on me as a toddler.

The rape incident happened when I was a toddler, and the memory had lain dormant for fifty years. I never had any thought of it until a teacher in the adult education class I was taking said, "today we will talk about secrets." All of a sudden, I felt flushed and began to quietly cry. I couldn't believe this reaction for I am a composed person, not easily brought to tears. The teacher noticed my behavior and asked me to join her outside the classroom. In the hall, she asked me if I was in therapy and I told her yes. She strongly suggested that I leave the class, go home, and call the therapist to make an appointment for that day. I couldn't believe what was happening and firmly told her I was fine and would be fine. "No," she said. "I want you to go now and promise me you will call her." I reluctantly left. In the car, I began playing over again the classroom situation and wondered what that was all about. I decided I would follow her advice.

When I got home, I made the phone call and was surprisingly able to get an appointment later that afternoon. I had been meeting with this therapist for over a year and had a trusted relationship with her.

That day as I shared with the therapist about the class experience, I gradually began to reveal what the word secret meant to me. The abuser was a male secretary who worked for my dad in the basement of our home for several years when I was very young. He had made me promise that I would never tell anyone what happened. He said, "The garbage men will take you away if anyone knows about our secret."

I remembered as a child being fearful of the garbage men and hiding in my closet if I heard them near our house. Even as an adult I felt uncomfortable when I heard the garbage truck coming, but I never knew why. I never told anyone about the incident until that moment with the therapist. My mind totally blocked it out. I remembered the playfulness of the abuser and how he would tease me. I interpreted it as his love for me. Our family even socialized with him and his wife.

Over the next few weeks and months after that therapy session, I got in touch progressively with my suppressed anger at the abuser, my parents not protecting me and never knowing about it, and the Blessed Virgin Mary who we as a family had a strong devotion to. Then, finally, I was able to blame God for allowing this to happen. It took several years for my emotional and spiritual healing. I had to be given permission to be *angry* with God from my Christian therapist. This sounded scary to me but I trusted her.

I will never forget my anger and rage as I scribbled the emotions onto two large manila papers, with a thick, kindergarten-sized, black crayon in my hand. I was on my knees, in our basement, furiously attacking the paper, black stripes back and forth, tears streaming down my face. I don't know how long I was down there but I was totally spent. Never had I experienced such emotion. I was drained and exhausted.

Several sessions later, my Christian therapist suggested that I needed to *forgive* God. I told her I would think about it. Forgiving God was foreign for me. I had forgiven *people* for incidents, but the thought of my needing to forgive God for allowing this childhood rape to happen was beyond me. I was told this exercise was for me, not God. I needed to forgive God, and I eventually did.

That was a turning point in my relationship with God the Father who I have now come to respect and love. I needed major surgery with Him. It wasn't until I compiled twenty years' worth of all my underlined scripture verses in my Jerusalem Bible that I came to see God the Father's unconditional love. Over and over again I had highlighted verses of "I forgive you" and "I love you." There were a few others, but mostly they were of forgiveness and love. God's love for me was the startling message. That's when my attitude toward God changed from one of a harsh God to one of a loving Father.

With time, I came to see that year after year I had been guided, even when I turned my back on God's love. He has continued to be there for me, inviting me back into His loving arms.

Facing the Fear:
God

Acknowledge:
Through mid-life talking and listening to people I learned it is okay to be angry with God. Growing up, I wouldn't dare feel this way. I realized that from some of the Bible readings, I feared God. I thought that if I didn't love God all the time, I would be banished to hell. I needed permission from the Christian therapist that it was okay to *wrestle* with God.

Write:
I have written letters to God and written what I thought were His replies. And I know by the peace in my heart that God still loves me.

Embrace:
Taking time in meditation brings me a sense of serenity. What I have learned is that I need to be honest with God and He does still love me.

Fears dissolve in action. Action gives me freedom. Freedom to fall into the hands of my loving God. For all this I am thankful. Amen.

Fear of Aging

Turning eighty... was I fearful? I sure didn't want to think about becoming eighty. I wanted to celebrate my birthday as I have for many of my decade entrances, but I didn't like the number. I have friends who are in their eighties with various health limitations and happy dispositions. It wasn't about them. It was about not having any idea of what life would hold for me going forward. What would I do with my life? I didn't have a plan, and I like plans.

Thinking ahead, the concept of senior life with so many possible variances of health and limited opportunities began to cloud my positive attitude. I was noticing more infirm people walking slowly, some with canes and some just being elderly.

For many weeks before the big day, I noticed a man in my neighborhood, day after day, sitting in a chair in his front yard, just looking out. "What is he looking at?" I would wonder. It was a scary thought for me. I know I shouldn't judge people, but I kept wondering what it was that entertained him.

I love to read, do puzzles, play tennis, walk, and have conversations with neighbors. I couldn't fathom just sitting in stillness. Then I think of the minutes meditating in my room. That is different to me. It is inside with my eyes closed. I definitely had a problem judging him. Is that what life was going to be like for me going forward? Slowing down and having limited activity seems to be my issue.

For weeks before the grand day, I pondered my attitudes. I talked with friends and inquired what it was like for them. None of them seemed to share my fear. As a matter of fact, they were all very encouraging, sharing their opinions.

At fifty, I also came to a crossroads, just like now. What would I do with my life going forward? I didn't have a plan then or any ideas. This was a similar feeling of unrest and now, I was also adding health to the equation.

During my early fifties, I spent a few years being especially observant to what my God might have wanted me to see. I went on a number of silent retreats, hoping God would reveal to me the master plan. It didn't happen that way. It unfolded gradually, and little did I realize how full my next thirty years would be, which I loved.

All my activities are put on the calendar, which I save. It wasn't until I was chronicling my life that I saw the whole picture of involvements these past thirty years: Spiritual Director training, Artist's Way course, autobiography writing, openness to art, facilitating writing groups. What beautiful surprises I was given. Never would I have planned or guessed how I would be guided.

Beginning my day with prayer, meditation, exercise, and journaling was a gift inviting me to be at peace most days. When I felt unsettled about something, I would pick up my pen to unearth the turmoil. Afterward, talking it over with a friend helped to settle me. I mention all this activity to point out that God gifted me with a plan that I had no idea about initially.

Journaling is definitely my tool of discovery. I decided before my big day that it would be helpful to see what was so unsettling. It seemed to me I kept talking in circles and felt frustrated. And so I began journaling on the *fear of turning eighty*. When I finished writing, I read it to my friend who knows me well.

"Jane, how is what you have written any different from what you have been living these past years?" As I was reading it to her, I was aware of the same realization. I told her, "It isn't any different. I want to continue doing what I have been doing."

"Then Jane, what is the big deal?" I explained to her I had felt stuck and just needed to face the intersection and move on down the road. I felt immense peace after that.

Once again, the tool of writing, using the *ANGER (feelings) QUESTIONS* found at the back of the book proved to be the gift of enlightenment. Over and over again I have used this tool to help me get unstuck. Writing and sharing my writings with a trusted friend is such a freeing gift.

The process doesn't take me longer than fifteen minutes usually. I address my feelings in the situation, and writing generally brings the confusion to a completion for me. I typically feel relieved after answering the questions and am guided by my pen, bringing me peace. I wish I remembered who gave me the questions, but my gray hairs have blocked this memory. Just know they have been a tremendous gift to me.

I am continuing to begin my day in prayer and do some sort of exercise that guides and enhances my life. Life has changed with the Covid virus pandemic limiting my activity, however, I am at peace responding to God's nudges each day. I am grateful for the health I have been given and the people God has put on my path. My life is a gift for which I am most grateful.

Facing the Fear:

Aging

Acknowledge:

Since writing has been an enlightening tool for me, I took up my pen once again. As a matter of fact, I know that I journaled many times, looking at my attitudes regarding health, activities, and death. It was a very unsettling time for me. What all my writing showed me was I didn't have a plan for the future and that was okay.

Write:

When I was twelve years old, I wrote in my diary that I wanted to be a secretary, get married, and have a large family. This was my deepest desire, and it all happened. I am most grateful. That was the beginning of *me* having a plan, and now I attempt to accept life as it unfolds, writing my way through it all.

Embrace:

As I wrote and shared my reflections with my Spiritual Director, it became a gift to me to see how I don't have to have a master plan.

My Closing Thoughts

Despite having written this book, I still have to remind myself that the only way to honor my fear is by acknowledging it, walking through it, and embracing it.

Walking literally helps me to process my emotions, especially when they are new and strong. Years ago my husband and I had a meeting with one of our children who was going through some introspection about how she was raised. Once I got home, I didn't know how to process my strong feelings, so I went for a power walk to work through my emotions.

Exercise and nature calm me. The walk helped me express my tangled feelings in a safe and therapeutic way. I was filled to the brim, ready to boil over, and this commune with nature worked out my overwhelming emotions. It didn't end there; I still needed to do a lot of writing, but the walk brought me to a point of settling down.

I am most grateful for all the guidance I have been given through my years with art as therapy, psychotherapy, writing therapy, special friends, and wisdom figures.

Taking action is the key to overcoming my fears. My healing experiences have taken time. I have had to be gentle with myself.

I have come to see how my fears want to control my actions, hold me back from freedom. It is when I live in fear that I live a limited life. I don't want to be tied down. I want the happiness and peace that come from walking through my fears. In conclusion, I say:

Thank you, God, for guiding and walking with me through these fears and encouraging me to live a JOY FILLED life. AMEN.

Anger (feelings) Questions

- What makes me angry?
- What is the real issue here?
- What do I *think* and *feel?*
- What do I want accomplished?
- Who is responsible for what?
- What do I want to change?
- What are the things I *will* and *will not* do?

About the Author

Jane Kucera wrote her autobiography, *Seasons of My Heart, Life is a Struggle but the Payoff is Worth it.* She also wrote *Taking Off My God Hat.* It is a compilation of scripture verses regarding forgiveness that impacted her life. The two art and poetry books sitting on her living room table are a reminder of her artistic past-times. Jane is a spiritual director who loves nature, walking, and playing tennis. She is blessed with her husband of fifty-nine years, eight children, nineteen grandchildren and one great-grandchild. What a fulfilling life!

Made in United States
North Haven, CT
25 August 2022

23220422R10043